DISCOVERING THE UNITED STATES

Hawaii

BY IB LARSEN

Kids Core

An Imprint of Abdo Publishing
abdobooks.com

abdobooks.com

Published by Abdo Publishing, a division of ABDO, PO Box 398166, Minneapolis, Minnesota 55439.

Printed in China.
052024
092024

Cover Photo: iStockphoto
Interior Photos: Christian Petersen/Getty Images for Ironman/Getty Images Sport/Getty Images, 4–5; Sean M. Haffey/Getty Images for Ironman/Getty Images Sport/Getty Images, 6; Shutterstock Images, 7, 9, 16, 20–21, 23, 25, 29 (bottom left); Steve Heap/Shutterstock Images, 10 (top left); Forest and Kim Starr/Flickr, 10 (top right); Margrit Hirsch/Shutterstock Images, 10 (bottom left); Denis Moskvinov/Shutterstock Images, 10 (bottom right); ilbusca/DigitalVision Vectors/Getty Images, 12–13; H. Armstrong Roberts/ClassicStock/Archive Photos/Getty Images, 14; Russ Bishop/Alamy, 18; MN Studio/Shutterstock Images, 22, 29 (bottom right); Damien Verrier/Shutterstock Images, 26; Red Line Editorial, 28 (top), 29 (top); Shane Myers Photography/Shutterstock Images, 28 (bottom)

Editor: Haley Williams
Series Designer: Katharine Hale

Library of Congress Control Number: 2023949339

Publisher's Cataloging-in-Publication Data

Names: Larsen, Ib, author.
Title: Hawaii / by Ib Larsen
Description: Minneapolis, Minnesota: Abdo Publishing, 2025 | Series: Discovering the United States | Includes online resources and index.
Identifiers: ISBN 9781098293819 (lib. bdg.) | ISBN 9798384913085 (ebook)
Subjects: LCSH: U.S. states--Juvenile literature. | Hawaii--History--Juvenile literature. | Western States (U.S.)--Juvenile literature. | Physical geography--United States--Juvenile literature.
Classification: DDC 973--dc23

All population data taken from:
"Estimates of Population by Sex, Race, and Hispanic Origin: April 1, 2020 to July 1, 2022." *US Census Bureau, Population Division*, June 2023, census.gov.

CONTENTS

Athletes need to be in very good shape to compete in the Ironman Triathlon.

The Big Race

It was February 18, 1978. The first Ironman Triathlon was about to begin in the state of Hawaii. A triathlon is a race where athletes swim, cycle, and run. But the Ironman Triathlon is different. Athletes swim 2.4 miles (3.9 km). They cycle 112 miles (180 km).

The United Kingdom's Lucy Charles-Barclay, *center*, won the women's Ironman World Championship in 2023.

Then they run 26.2 miles (42.2 km). These distances are longer than in other triathlons.

Fifteen athletes competed in the first Ironman Triathlon. All day, they kicked through ocean water. They pedaled their bikes. And they ran on city streets. Not every competitor completed the race. Three people dropped out before the finish line. Gordon Haller was the first to finish. He completed the race in 11 hours and 46 minutes.

Hawaii's flag features eight stripes. They represent the state's eight main islands.

The Ironman World Championship is usually held in Hawaii every year. It has become one of the world's biggest triathlons. In 2023, more than 2,000 athletes competed in the race. People can watch the race on television. Or they can visit Hawaii and see it in person.

Hawaii's Land

Hawaii is located in the Pacific Ocean. It is made up of eight big islands and 124 smaller ones. The largest is the island of Hawaii. It is often called the Big Island. The next three biggest islands are Maui, Oahu, and Kauai. The islands formed about 70 million years ago due to volcanic eruptions.

How Did Volcanoes Make Hawaii?

Volcanic eruptions happen when **magma** from deep within Earth comes out onto the planet's surface. Over time, eruptions in the Pacific Ocean brought up a lot of magma. It cooled and became the islands of Hawaii. The 15 volcanoes that made the main islands are still there today.

Tunnels Beach on Kauai is named after the underwater caves found throughout the area. Many people enjoy snorkeling and scuba diving there.

Hawaii became the fiftieth US state in 1959. But it is very far from other states. Hawaii is about 2,300 miles (3,700 km) from California's coast.

Hawaii Facts

DATE OF STATEHOOD
August 21, 1959

CAPITAL
Honolulu

POPULATION
1,440,196

AREA
10,932 square miles
(28,314 sq km)

STATE BIRD

Nene

STATE TREE

Kukui tree

STATE FLOWER

Yellow hibiscus

STATE INDIVIDUAL SPORT

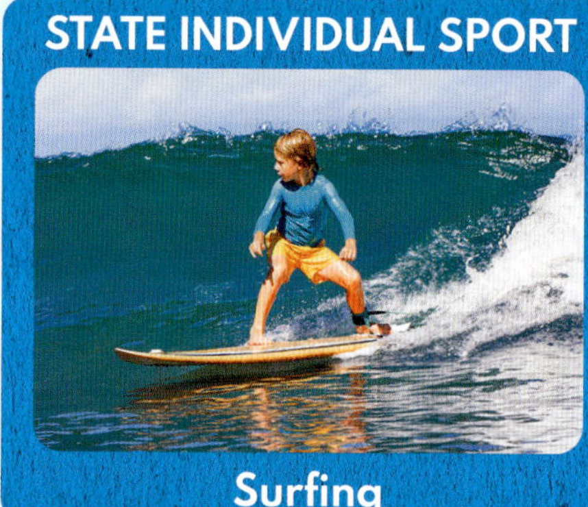

Surfing

Each US state has a different population, size, and capital city. States also have state symbols.

Hawaii has beautiful beaches on its islands. It also has tall mountains. Mauna Kea is the tallest at 13,796 feet (4,205 m). Bamboo forests cover parts of the state. Dolphins, whales, and sea turtles swim in its waters.

Hawaii's Climate

In most of Hawaii, there are only two seasons. Those seasons are summer and winter. Summers are warmer and drier than winters. In the winter, wind brings moisture from the ocean over the island. It falls as rain. Temperatures in the state vary with **elevation**. Hawaii's mountains are cooler than its beaches.

Further Evidence

Look at the website below. Does it give any new evidence to support Chapter One?

Hawaii

abdocorelibrary.com/discovering-hawaii

Native Hawaiians used to live in buildings made of wood, grasses, and leaves.

CHAPTER 2

The People of Hawaii

The first people in Hawaii came from other Pacific Islands. They arrived sometime between 300 and 600 CE. These people are known as Polynesians. Polynesia is a collection of more than 1,000 islands in the Pacific Ocean.

Many Native Hawaiians continue practicing important Hawaiian traditions, including hula dancing.

Over time, people in Hawaii began to develop their own culture. They built canoes and fished for food. They also made art and music.

Early white **settlers** came to Hawaii from the United States and Europe in the late 1700s. In the 1800s, people from China, Japan, and several other Asian countries arrived there. Many Hawaiians today come from these early **immigrants**.

In 2022, 37 percent of people in Hawaii were Asian. White people made up 21 percent of the population. About 10 percent were Native Hawaiians and other Pacific Islanders. Black people made up 2 percent, and about 11 percent were Hispanic or Latino.

Culture

Many people in Hawaii enjoy traditional Polynesian food. One popular food is poi. This is a paste made by pounding cooked **taro** root. The dish can be sweet or sour depending on how it is made.

Fish dishes such as poke (pronounced POH-kay) and lomi lomi salmon are very common in Hawaii.

Another popular dish is lau lau. It is made by wrapping pork in taro leaves and cooking it underground. Some people like to eat poi and lau lau together.

Hawaii is known for the sport of surfing. People have been surfing in Hawaii since before European settlers arrived. Today, many surfing competitions are held in the state every year.

Some famous people come from Hawaii. Former US president Barack Obama is from Oahu. So is the singer Bruno Mars.

Hula

Hula dancing is a big part of Hawaiian culture. It is an art form that has been practiced on Hawaii for hundreds of years. Hula is a kind of storytelling told through dance and movement. It is one way Native Hawaiians can share their knowledge, history, and culture with others.

Kauai Coffee Company is the largest coffee grower in the United States.

Industry

Hawaii gets a lot of tourists every year. So, many people in the state have jobs in hotels, restaurants, and parks. Other people have jobs growing crops such as sugarcane and coffee. Some also raise cattle. Many members of the US military are in Hawaii as well. This is because there are 14 military bases throughout the islands.

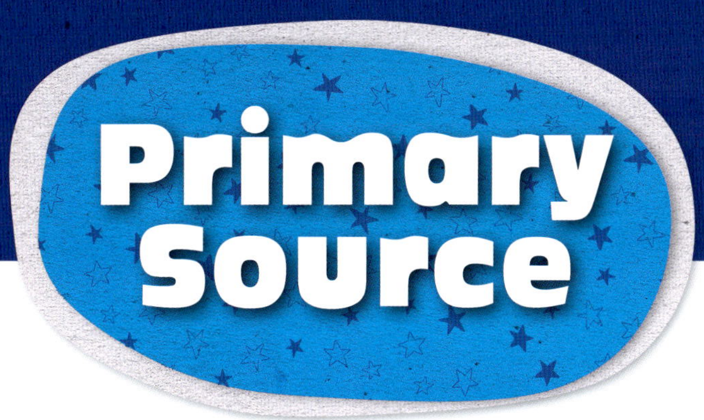

Surfer Ha'a Keaulana spoke about how surfing is a big part of Native Hawaiian culture:

> [Surfing is] our church, because that's where we spiritually can connect to something that was always there as Native Hawaiians. I feel connected to my **ancestors**. I feel connected to my culture.

Source: Becky Worley, et al. "New Wave of Hawaiian Surfers Look to Reclaim Sport's Cultural Spirit." *ABC News*, 1 June 2023, abcnews.go.com. Accessed 5 Sept. 2023.

What's the Big Idea?

Read this quote carefully. What is its main idea? Explain how the main idea is supported by details.

Waikiki Beach in Honolulu is one of the most popular beaches in Hawaii.

Places in Hawaii

The capital of Hawaii is Honolulu. Honolulu is also the state's biggest city. It is on the island of Oahu. The largest city on Maui is Kahului. Hilo is the biggest city on the Big Island. On the island of Kauai, the largest city is Kapaa.

The Pipiwai Trail is a popular place to hike in Haleakalā National Park. The trail cuts through a bamboo forest and leads to the Makahiku and Waimoku waterfalls.

Parks

Some of Hawaii's most beautiful locations are in its parks. Haleakalā National Park is on the island of Maui. It is named after the giant volcano in the park. Some plants and animals in the park are very rare. These include the nene bird and the Haleakalā silversword plant.

Another national park in the state is Hawai'i Volcanoes National Park. This park is on the

Hawai'i Volcanoes National Park is open 24 hours a day, so visitors can see magma flowing from the Kilauea volcano even at night.

Big Island. The two volcanoes there are Mauna Loa and Kilauea. Visitors can hike on trails that go through the park.

Hawaii also has many wonderful state parks. Waimea Canyon State Park is on the island of Kauai. The canyon the park is named after is 1 mile (1.6 km) wide and more than 3,500 feet (1,067 m) deep. People visit the park to look over the canyon's edge.

The Road to Hana

The Road to Hana is a scenic highway on the island of Maui. The 52-mile (84-km) highway connects the towns of Kahului and Hana. It has more than 600 curves and can take several hours to drive. The Upper Waikani Falls is one of many landmarks people can visit along the Road to Hana.

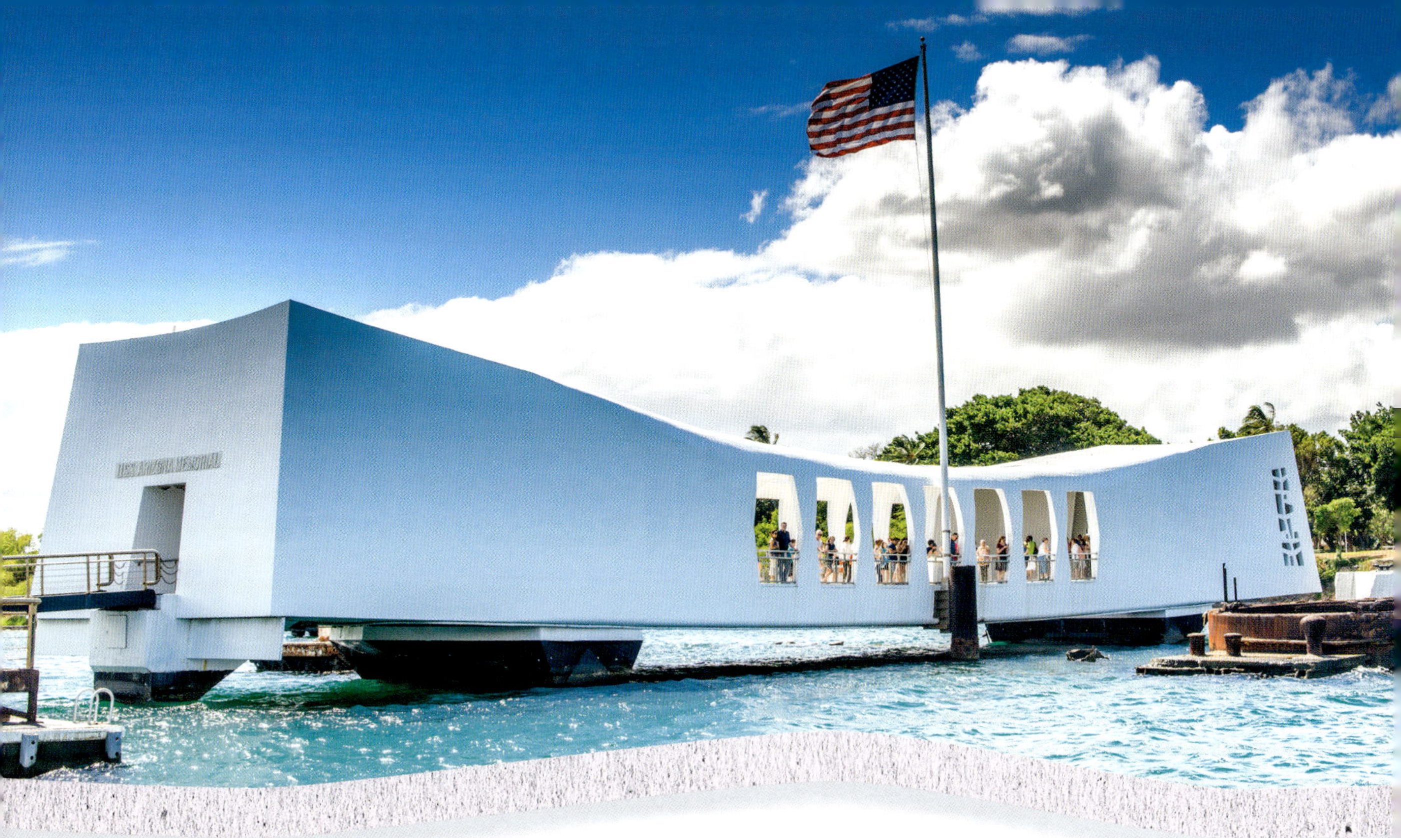

A memorial was built where the USS *Arizona* ship sank after it was bombed during the Pearl Harbor attack.

Landmarks

Pearl Harbor is one of Hawaii's most famous landmarks. It is on the island of Oahu. It contains a military base for the US Navy. On December 7, 1941, the Empire of Japan attacked the base at Pearl Harbor. This brought the United States into World War II (1939–1945).

Wood carvings known as ki'i symbolize the Hawaiian gods. Many people visit the Royal Grounds in Pu'uhonua o Hōnaunau National Historical Park to see the ki'i there.

Another famous landmark is Iolani Palace. It is on Oahu. Hawaiian **royalty** lived in the palace from 1882 to 1893. Visitors can go there to learn more about the history of Hawaii.

Hawaii's natural beauty and interesting history attract many visitors every year. People can swim in Hawaii's waters and hike through its parks. They can visit its cities and towns. And they can learn about Native Hawaiian culture. There are many amazing things people can do in the state of Hawaii.

Explore Online

Visit the website below. Does it give any new information about Hawai'i Volcanoes National Park that wasn't in Chapter Three?

Hawai'i Volcanoes National Park

abdocorelibrary.com/discovering-hawaii

State Map

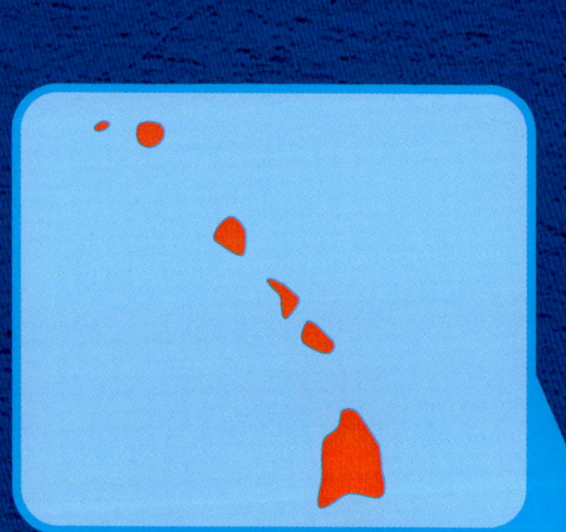

Waimea Canyon State Park

Hawaii: The Aloha State

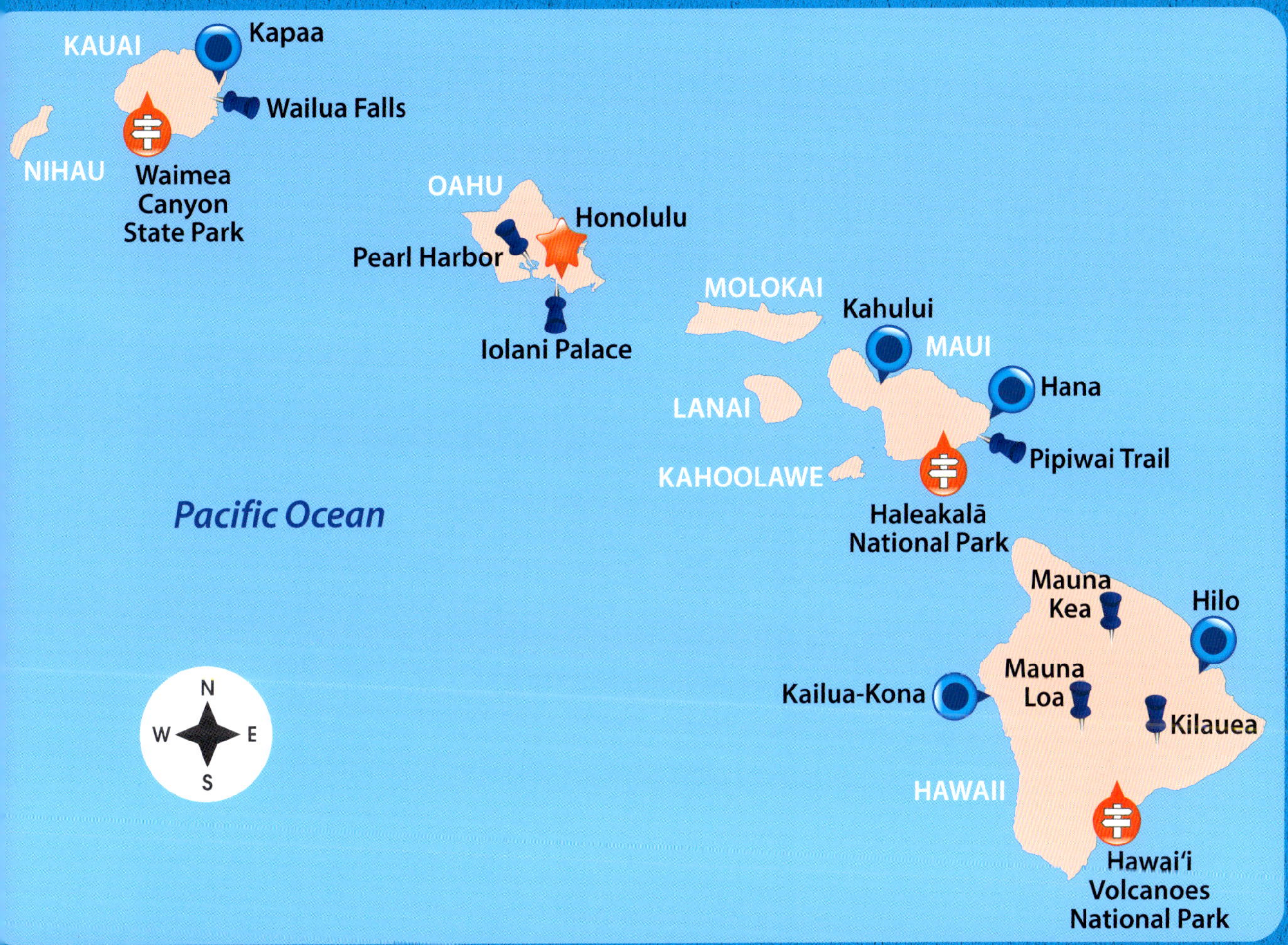

KAUAI
Kapaa
Wailua Falls
NIHAU
Waimea Canyon State Park
OAHU
Honolulu
Pearl Harbor
Iolani Palace
MOLOKAI
Kahului
MAUI
Hana
LANAI
Pipiwai Trail
KAHOOLAWE
Haleakalā National Park
Pacific Ocean
Mauna Kea
Hilo
Mauna Loa
Kailua-Kona
Kilauea
HAWAII
Hawai'i Volcanoes National Park
N
W
E
S

Wailua Falls

Pipiwai Trail

Glossary

ancestors
the people from whom a person is descended and who lived many generations ago

elevation
the height above sea level

immigrants
people who move to a different country

magma
hot, liquid material beneath Earth's surface

royalty
a class of people who have power in a country, such as kings, queens, or emperors and their families

settlers
people who moved to a new area

taro
a root vegetable commonly eaten in Asia, Africa, and the Pacific Islands

Online Resources

To learn more about Hawaii, visit our free resource websites below.

Visit **abdocorelibrary.com** or scan this QR code for free Common Core resources for teachers and students, including vetted activities, multimedia, and booklinks, for deeper subject comprehension.

Visit **abdobooklinks.com** or scan this QR code for free additional online weblinks for further learning. These links are routinely monitored and updated to provide the most current information available.

Learn More

Katz, Susan B. *The History of Pearl Harbor: A World War II Book for New Readers*. Rockridge, 2021.

Scheff, Matt. *Surfing*. Abdo, 2021.

Tieck, Sarah. *Hawaii*. Abdo, 2020.

Index

About the Author

Ib Larsen is a writer and editorial assistant living in Saint Paul, Minnesota.